I0813167

DISCOVERING THE UNITED STATES

Washington, DC

BY KATHY MACMILLAN

An Imprint of Abdo Publishing
abdobooks.com

abdobooks.com

Printed in China.
052024
092024

Cover Photo: Musa Visual Media LLC/Shutterstock Images
Interior Photos: AFP/Getty Images, 4–5; Orhan Cam/Shutterstock Images, 6; Jim E. Johnson/Shutterstock Images, 9 (top left); iStockphoto, 9 (top right); Shutterstock Images, 9 (bottom left), 14, 29 (bottom); Stephan Roeger/Shutterstock Images, 9 (bottom right); MH Anderson Photography/Shutterstock Images, 10; Joseph Gruber/Alamy, 12–13; Laurence Griffiths/Getty Images Sport/Getty Images, 17; Vitor Munhoz/National Hockey League/Getty Images, 18; Jon Bilous/Shutterstock Images, 20–21; Sean Pavone/Shutterstock Images, 23, 24, 28 (Lincoln Memorial); Giuseppe Crimeni/Shutterstock Images, 26; Red Line Editorial, 28 (map); Robert A. Powell/Shutterstock Images, 28 (Rock Creek Park); Red Line Editorial/CrossroadsCreative/DigitalVision Vectors/Getty Images, 29 (top)

Editor: Marley Richmond
Series Designer: Katharine Hale

Library of Congress Control Number: 2023949378

Publisher's Cataloging-in-Publication Data

Names: MacMillan, Kathy, author.
Title: Washington, DC / by Kathy MacMillan
Description: Minneapolis, Minnesota: Abdo Publishing, 2025 | Series: Discovering the United States | Includes online resources and index.
Identifiers: ISBN 9781098294199 (lib. bdg.) | ISBN 9798384913467 (ebook)
Subjects: LCSH: U.S. states--Juvenile literature. | Washington (D.C.)--History--Juvenile literature. | Southeastern States--Juvenile literature. | Physical geography--United States--Juvenile literature.
Classification: DDC 973--dc23

All population data taken from:
"Estimates of Population by Sex, Race, and Hispanic Origin: April 1, 2020 to July 1, 2022." *US Census Bureau, Population Division*, June 2023, census.gov.

CONTENTS

On August 28, 1963, people gathered in Washington, DC. Martin Luther King Jr. delivered his famous speech to the crowd.

CHAPTER 1

A City of Tradition and Change

August 28, 1963, was a hot day in Washington, DC. But more than 250,000 people gathered along the National Mall and near the Lincoln Memorial. In 1963, Black Americans faced **discrimination**. Schools, train cars, and even bathrooms were segregated.

The United States Capitol building is in Washington, DC. This is where many US government officials work.

That meant Black and white people were separated in those places. So people had come from all over the country for a peaceful **protest**.

Speakers called on lawmakers to make fairer laws. They wanted Black Americans to have the same rights and opportunities as white Americans.

Martin Luther King Jr. spoke last. King was a famous civil rights **activist**. He had stayed up all night writing his speech. But halfway through it, he put aside his notes. He spoke from his heart. His speech honored the hopes of the nation's founders. But it also called for changes to make life fairer for all Americans.

City and District

Washington, DC, is different from other cities. It is the capital of the United States. It is not a part of any state.

Washington, DC, is a federal district. *DC* stands for District of Columbia. The US Congress makes laws for DC directly. DC also has a local government. But it does not have as much power as US state governments. The US government owns about half of the land in DC.

Where to Put the Capital

Choosing the location of the US capital was difficult for the US government. Ultimately, President George Washington chose the location for Washington, DC. Maryland and Virginia both gave land to make the city. In 1846, Virginia got its portion of land back. DC is now made entirely of land that was formerly Maryland.

Washington, DC, Facts

DATE OF FOUNDING
July 16, 1790

POPULATION
671,803

AREA
68 square miles (176 sq km)

OFFICIAL BIRD

Wood thrush

OFFICIAL TREE

Scarlet oak

OFFICIAL FLOWER

American Beauty rose

OFFICIAL FRUIT

Cherry

Each US state and district has a different population and size. States and districts also have official symbols.

A Place on the Potomac

Washington, DC, is bordered by two states. Maryland is to the northwest, northeast, and southeast. Virginia borders DC to the southwest.

The trees in DC turn bright colors during autumn.

DC sits on the Potomac River. The land near the river is flat. But the district is surrounded by hills.

DC is home to many plants and animals. Oaks and maples are the city's most common trees. More than 240 different kinds of birds live in the city. They include bald eagles, blue jays, ducks, and hawks. Squirrels, opossums, foxes, and groundhogs also live in DC.

DC has a moderate climate. It has four seasons. Winters are cold and wet. But it does not snow often. Summers are hot and **humid**. Autumn and spring temperatures are mild. The city gets plenty of rain all year long.

Further Evidence

Look at the website below. Does it give any new evidence to support Chapter One?

Washington, DC

abdocorelibrary.com/discovering-washington-dc

Anacostans fished in the Anacostia River for food. They also farmed on land near the river.

CHAPTER 2

The People of Washington, DC

People first came to the land that is now Washington, DC, at least 4,000 years ago. More than 12 different American Indian peoples have lived in the area. The Anacostans lived along the Anacostia River. They traded goods with other peoples.

DC's flag is based on George Washington's coat of arms. This was a symbol that represented his family.

The Piscataway peoples also lived in the area. They grew crops, hunted, and fished. European settlers pushed Piscataway people off their land in the 1600s and 1700s. Today, many Piscataway people live in Maryland.

Washington, DC, Today

Today, more than 670,000 people live in DC. Black people make up 45 percent of the population. About 37 percent of DC residents are white. Almost 12 percent are Hispanic or Latino. Nearly 5 percent are Asian. Less than 1 percent are American Indian.

Deaf Community in DC

Gallaudet University is the only university in the world for deaf and hard of hearing students. Students come from all over the nation and from other countries. It is common to see people using sign language in the city. DC has many Deaf-owned businesses.

Washington, DC, has many embassies. These are places where **representatives** from other countries work. More than 168 languages are spoken in the city.

Several famous people come from DC. Olympic swimmer Katie Ledecky was born there. So was basketball player Kevin Durant.

Culture and Jobs

The food in DC comes from all over the world. Many people in the city love spicy smoked sausages called half-smokes. Blue crabs are also popular. They come from the nearby Chesapeake Bay.

Baseball, football, and hockey are DC's most popular sports. Fans of the Washington

Katie Ledecky won two gold medals and two silver medals in the 2020 Olympic Games in Tokyo, Japan.

Nationals baseball team can see the US Capitol building from the team's stadium. During football season, fans cheer on the Washington Commanders. The Washington Capitals are DC's professional ice hockey team.

Fans cheer for the Washington Capitals hockey team.

Many people in DC work for the US government. They help make laws. They run programs that support people all over the country. Other people have jobs in technology, education, and health care.

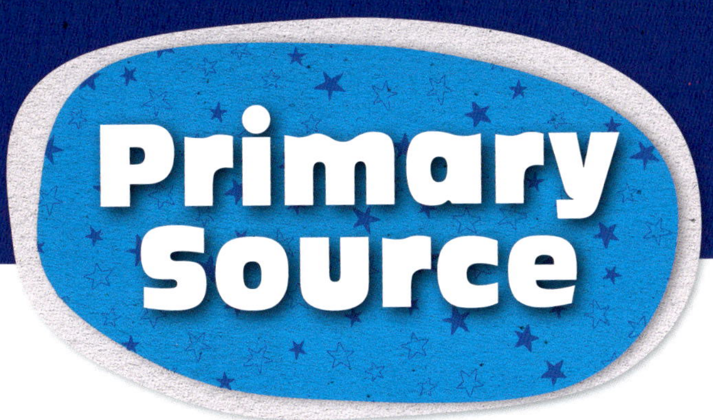

Katharine Graham was head of the DC newspaper the *Washington Post*. This is how she described DC:

> It is a city that offers me more people—more different kinds of people—than I could otherwise possibly have come to know in a lifetime.

Source: Katharine Graham. *Katharine Graham's Washington.* Vintage Books, 2022, p. 3.

Comparing Texts

Think about the quote. Does it support the information in this chapter? Or does it give a different perspective? Explain how in a few sentences.

Georgetown is known for its historic row houses. Many were built in the mid-1700s.

CHAPTER 3

Places in Washington, DC

Washington, DC, has 132 different neighborhoods. The oldest is Georgetown. The Shaw neighborhood is a center of African American culture. Howard University is in Shaw. It is a historically Black university.

The most famous part of DC is Capitol Hill. The US Congress makes laws there in the US Capitol building. The US Supreme Court is there too. So is the Library of Congress. This is the largest library in the world. The White House is near Capitol Hill. The president of the United States lives there.

The National Cherry Blossom Festival

In 1912, the mayor of Tokyo, Japan, gave 3,000 cherry trees to Washington, DC. The city holds a celebration each spring when the trees blossom. The National Cherry Blossom Festival lasts for four weeks. People celebrate with a parade, music, and fireworks.

In the early spring, cherry trees bloom near the Washington Monument in DC.

Monuments

The National Mall is an open park. It has many memorials. One is the Washington Monument. This **obelisk** honors George Washington.

Visitors can see the world's largest collection of historic aircraft at the National Air and Space Museum.

Visitors can ride an elevator to the top to see the whole city.

The Lincoln Memorial honors President Abraham Lincoln. It has 36 tall columns. The statue of Lincoln inside is 19 feet (5.8 m) high.

More Places to See

The Smithsonian Institution has many free museums in DC. The National Air and Space Museum teaches about the history of flight. It displays many planes and spacecraft. Visitors can even touch a rock from the moon.

The National Museum of the American Indian tells the story of American Indians from the past to today. Visitors learn about American Indian history, toys, art, and more.

At the National Museum of Natural History, visitors can see **fossils** and Egyptian mummies. They can learn about how Earth has changed over time. Exhibits also teach visitors about interesting animals. Many of these animals are now **extinct**.

The US Holocaust Memorial Museum displays images of Holocaust victims in order to remember and honor them.

The US Holocaust Memorial Museum is also in DC. During World War II (1939–1945), Germany's Nazi Party killed more than 6 million Jewish people. This is known as the Holocaust.

The museum tells the story of the Holocaust. It features three floors of exhibits.

Washington, DC, is a place that honors history. But it is also a city of today. Laws made in DC affect the whole country. People come from all over the world to DC. They bring their art and culture with them. DC is always changing and growing.

Explore Online

Visit the website below. Does it give any new information about the White House that wasn't in Chapter Three?

Virtual Tour of the White House

abdocorelibrary.com/discovering-washington-dc

District Map

KEY

Neighborhood

Park

Point of interest

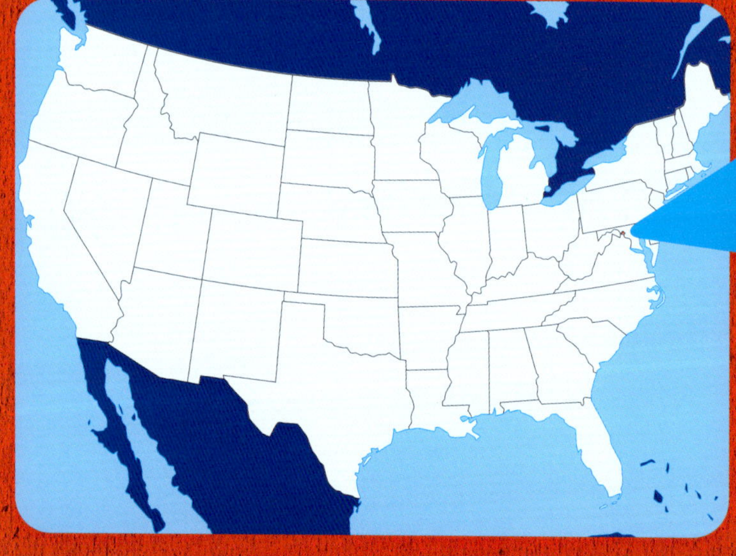

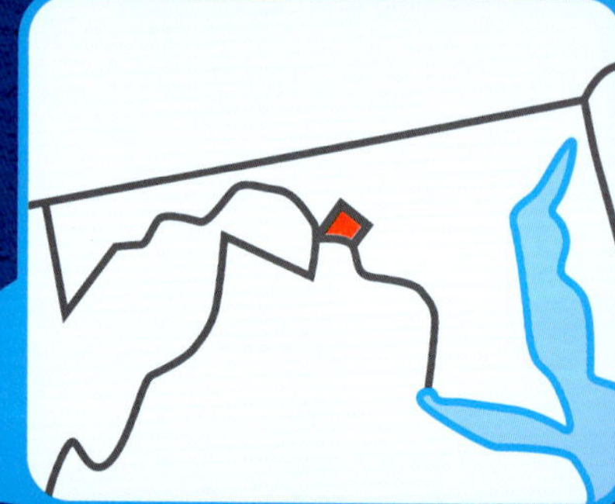

Rock Creek Park

Washington, DC: The Federal City

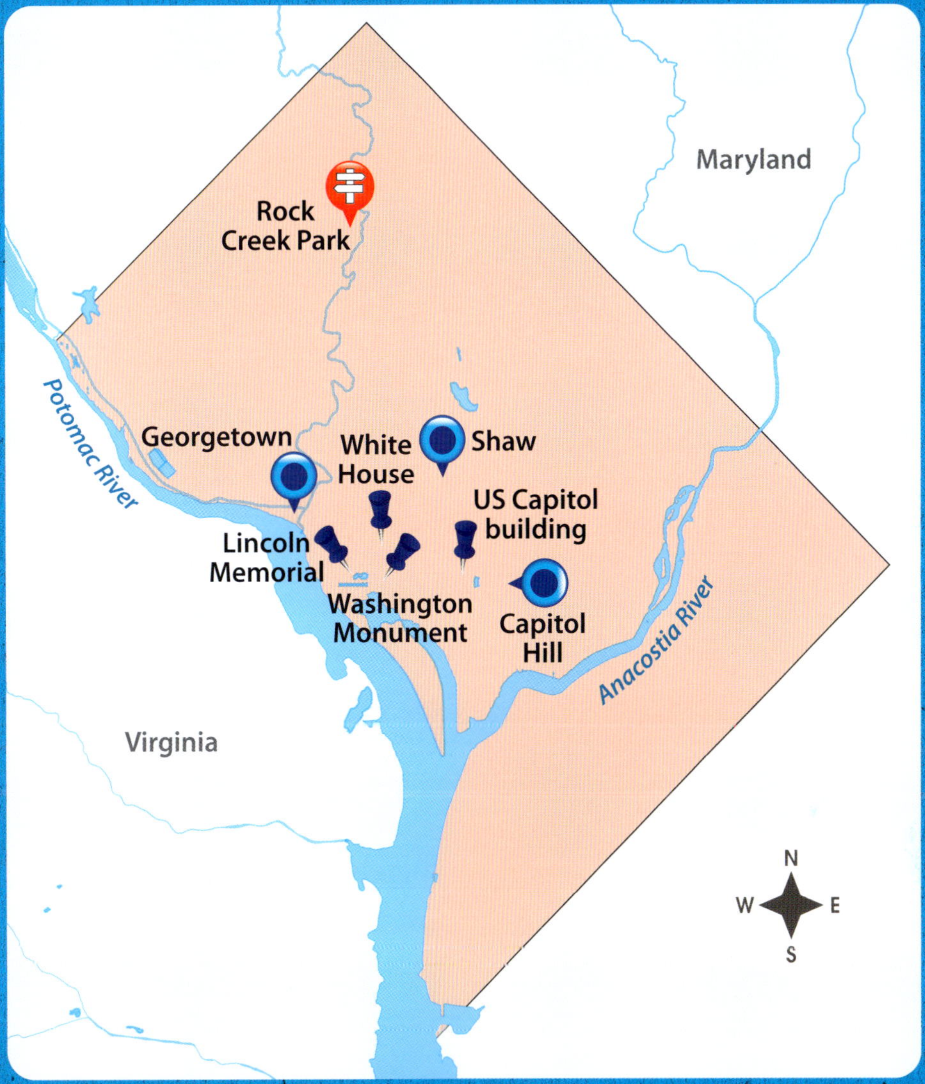

Maryland
Rock Creek Park
Potomac River
Georgetown
White House
Shaw
US Capitol building
Lincoln Memorial
Washington Monument
Capitol Hill
Anacostia River
Virginia
N
W
E
S

Lincoln Memorial

White House

Glossary

activist
a person who takes action to support a cause

discrimination
treating a person or group worse than others because of differences

extinct
no longer exists

fossils
the very old, preserved remains of animals or plants

humid
describing air that has a lot of moisture

obelisk
a tall, four-sided pillar with a pyramid shape at the top

protest
a statement or action to show disapproval of something

representatives
people who speak or act for a group

Online Resources

To learn more about Washington, DC, visit our free resource websites below.

Visit **abdocorelibrary.com** or scan this QR code for free Common Core resources for teachers and students, including vetted activities, multimedia, and booklinks, for deeper subject comprehension.

Visit **abdobooklinks.com** or scan this QR code for free additional online weblinks for further learning. These links are routinely monitored and updated to provide the most current information available.

Learn More

Carr, Aaron. *Washington Monument.* AV2, 2022.

Hewson, Anthony K. *Washington Nationals.* Abdo, 2023.

Tieck, Sarah. *Washington, DC.* Abdo, 2020.

Index

About the Author

Kathy MacMillan is a writer, nationally certified American Sign Language interpreter, librarian, and signing storyteller. She writes picture books, children's nonfiction, middle grade and young adult fiction, and resource books for educators and librarians. She went to college in Washington, DC. She lives in Baltimore, Maryland.